LIFE IN AN ESTUARY

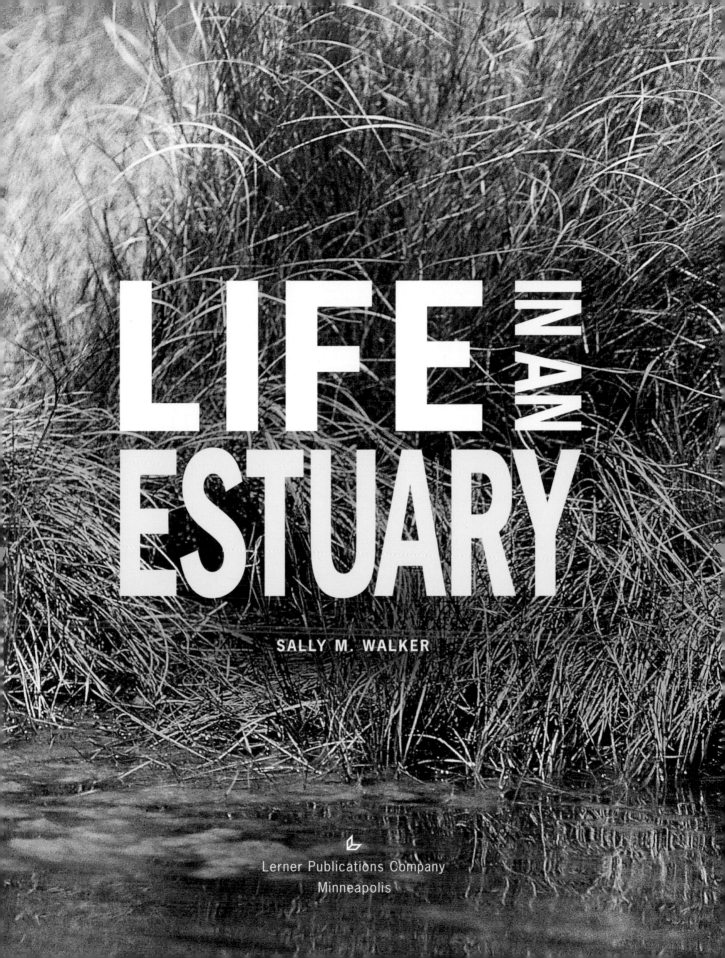

LIFE IN AN ESTUARY

SALLY M. WALKER

Lerner Publications Company
Minneapolis

For Jim, Erin, David, Donna, and Kippy
Thanks for all our lovely walks on sandy beaches, muddy tidal flats,
and winding salt marsh trails.

Lerner Publications Company
A division of Lerner Publishing Group
241 First Avenue North
Minneapolis, MN 55401 U.S.A.

Website address: www.lernerbooks.com

Library of Congress Cataloging-in-Publication Data

Walker, Sally M.
        Life in an estuary / by Sally Walker.
            p.   cm. — (Ecosystems in action)
        Includes bibliographical references (p.   ) and index.
        Summary: Examines the physical features, processes, and many different species of plants and animals that make up the ecosystem of the largest estuary in the United States, the Chesapeake Bay.
        ISBN: 0–8225–2137–7 (lib. bdg. : alk. paper)
        1. Estuarine biology—Juvenile literature.   2. Estuarine ecology—Juvenile literature.
        3. Estuaries—Juvenile literature.   [1. Chesapeake Bay (Md. and Va.)   2. Estuaries.
        3. Estuarine ecology.   4. Ecology.]   I. Title.   II. Series.
        QH95.9 .W35 2003
        577.7'8616347—dc21   2001006019

Manufactured in the United States of America
1 2 3 4 5 6 – JR – 08 07 06 05 04 03

CONTENTS

INTRODUCTION
WHAT IS AN ECOSYSTEM?

The next time you go outside, look closely at your surroundings. Buildings, streets, or people may be the first things you notice. But if you look and listen carefully, you may notice insects crawling or birds singing. Perhaps you'll see a squirrel munching an acorn in a nearby tree. Take a look at the plants. Are they tall and leafy or do they have prickly needles?

Now examine the soil. Is it dark and rich or filled with rocks? Is the air hot and humid or cool and dry? Do you think it will rain soon? When you look at living things or think about the environment they live in, you are exploring an ecosystem. An ecosystem is a specific community of organisms and their nonliving environment—the climate, soil, water, and air. Whether you live in a city, a suburb, or a rural area, your neighborhood is an ecosystem. The Sonoran Desert in the Southwest, the Everglades in Florida, and the Chesapeake Bay in Maryland and Virginia are also ecosystems.

Organisms survive by adapting to the physical conditions of their environment. Humans are highly adaptable organisms. We can build different kinds of homes for shelter, make clothing suitable for all weather conditions, and preserve food and transport it from place to place. These skills allow us to live in all kinds of ecosystems.

Some organisms can survive in only one kind of ecosystem. A saguaro cactus, for example, is adapted for life in hot, dry places. This prickly plant thrives in the Sonoran Desert, but it couldn't survive on the cold, windy, wet slopes of Alaska's Mount McKinley.

CHESAPEAKE BAY IS AN ECOSYSTEM

Earth has many different biomes, including forests, lakes, deserts, grasslands, and wetlands. Each ecosystem is a specific example of a biome. For example, Chesapeake Bay is an estuary—a body of water that occurs when a river carrying freshwater flows into a body of salt water. Many of the world's bays are estuaries. Chesapeake Bay is the largest estuary in the United States. Puget Sound in Washington, California's San Francisco Bay, Río de la Plata between Argentina and Uruguay, and the mouth of China's Yangtze River are also important estuaries.

An estuary is often fringed with wetlands. According to scientists, a wetland is any place where the water level is at or near the surface of the ground most of the year. Swamps, marshes, and bogs are wetlands too. Spanish moss drapes from towering cypress trees in the steamy, mysterious swamps in South Carolina, while a bog on a West Virginia mountaintop is open, breezy, and covered with small, wiry shrubs that can tolerate cold temperatures and strong winds.

Thousands of species of plants, animals, and other living things are born, grow, reproduce, die, and finally decay in an estuary and on the land that surrounds it. Living in an estuary and adapting to its many environmental conditions requires an enormous amount of energy. Energy moves through an ecosystem by way of its food chain. Food is the fuel that keeps organisms alive. A food chain is a feeding order that transfers energy from one species to another.

An estuary food chain begins with green plants and other primary producers. These organisms make food for themselves by absorbing energy

THOUSANDS OF SPECIES OF PLANTS, ANIMALS, AND OTHER LIVING THINGS ARE BORN, GROW, REPRODUCE, DIE, AND FINALLY DECAY IN AN ESTUARY AND ON THE LAND THAT SURROUNDS IT.

PRIMARY PRODUCERS: PROTOCTISTS

Algae, diatoms, and dinoflagellates are simple organisms that live in wet or moist places. These creatures are not animals or plants or fungi. They belong to a group of organisms known as protoctists.

Algae, diatoms, and dinoflagellates are widespread and abundant in estuary ecosystems. Thousands may be present in a single drop of water. Algae often anchor themselves to rocks, wood, and even shells, forming a slippery, slimy cover that may be green, brown, yellow, or red. Diatoms float in the water, at the mercy of the current. Some use threadlike structures to link themselves together, forming floating chains. Dinoflagellates use hairlike appendages called flagella to propel themselves through the water.

Like green plants, algae, diatoms, and dinoflagellates carry on photosynthesis and are important primary producers. A wide variety of shellfish and other estuary animals eat these protoctists. Still other animals consume the protoctist-eaters. Because algae, diatoms, and dinoflagellates use photosynthesis to manufacture food, they are sometimes referred to as photoplankton.

from sunlight and using it to power photosynthesis—a reaction in which carbon dioxide and water are converted into oxygen and glucose, a simple sugar. Some of the glucose is used to make starch, a substance that stores energy.

The energy in green plants and other primary producers passes into primary consumers when they eat the producers. For example, when a minnow nibbles on a water plant, the plant supplies the energy the minnow needs to live and grow. In turn, a larger fish—a secondary consumer that doesn't eat plants—gets its energy by gobbling up the minnow. When the larger fish dies and sinks to the bottom of the estuary, its body provides food for another group of life-forms called decomposers. These bacteria and fungi break down the fish's body and release nutrients, which may be taken up by plant roots. This is how energy and nutrients cycle through an estuary ecosystem.

In addition, new nutrients are constantly being carried into estuaries by the rivers that feed them. As a result, an estuary ecosystem usually has enough nutrients and energy to meet the high demands of its inhabitants.

For a long time, many people didn't realize how important estuaries are. Now we know that even creatures that live outside an estuary's ecosystem may depend on the estuary for their survival. How is an estuary, such as the Chesapeake Bay estuary, different from other watery ecosystems? What makes it so special and why should we protect it? Read on to find out.

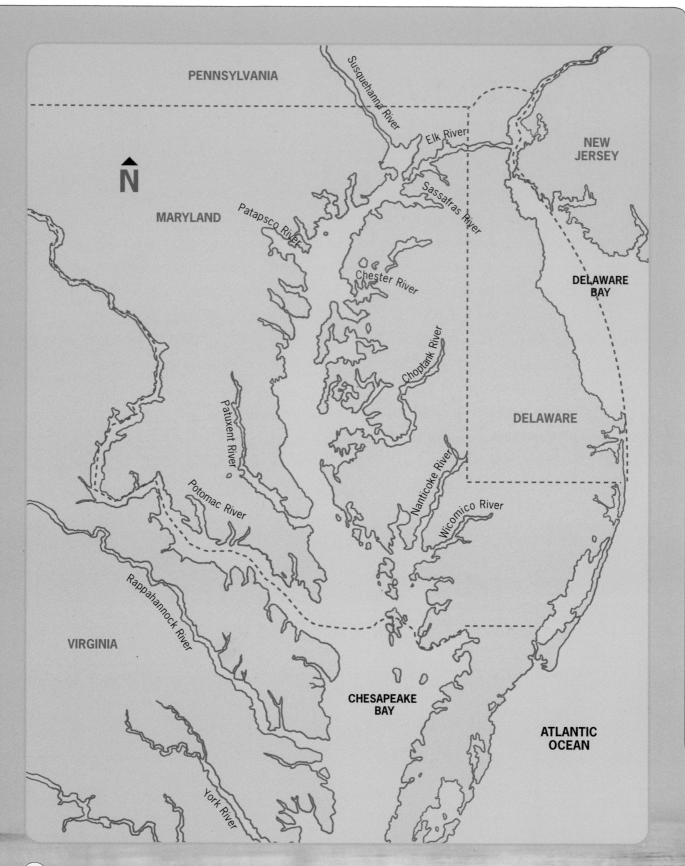

CHAPTER 1
THE CHESAPEAKE BAY:
A NATURAL HISTORY

About 35 million years ago, a meteoroid sped toward the earth. It streaked down through the atmosphere and smashed into the crust. The impact created a basin, or depression, that many years later would become the site of Chesapeake Bay. But before the bay formed, many other changes took place.

For millions of years, rain trickled down the rugged slopes of the Appalachian Mountains. As the small rivulets rolled over rock and soil, they combined to form creeks and streams. Flowing downhill toward the east, they formed larger streams and then rushing rivers that tumbled over rocky cliffs and pounded the earth below. The rivers swept up sediment—rocks, pebbles, and soil—and carried it along on their seaward journey. The rivers became larger and wider as new streams joined them. As time passed, water currents dug the river channels wider and deeper.

Once the rivers reached flatter ground, their currents slowed and spilled out across

THE APPALACHIAN MOUNTAINS

the land. No longer constantly swirling in fast currents, sediment began to settle. Over millions of years, the many layers of sediment formed a widespread coastal plain. As rivers flowed across the plain, their currents carved V-shaped valleys.

THE SUSQUEHANNA RIVER

The Susquehanna River begins in Lake Otsego in the Appalachian Mountains of New York State. The river flows southwest through central New York and then winds its way south across the eastern part of Pennsylvania. Along the way, many streams and smaller rivers flow into the Susquehanna. Eventually, the river reaches the coastal plains of northern Maryland and then empties into Chesapeake Bay.

At one time, the Susquehanna River followed a different course. It flowed farther south across the coastal plain and emptied into the Atlantic Ocean close to the border between Virginia and North Carolina. What happened to this ancient river valley? As odd as it may sound, the river valley was drowned. This part of the Susquehanna River's story involves not water, but ice.

HERONS (*ARDEA*) PERCH ON ROCKS IN THE SUSQUEHANNA RIVER.

During the Pleistocene Epoch—a geologic time period that began about 2 million years ago and ended about 12,000 years ago—thick, moving sheets of ice called glaciers spread across the land. At times, glaciers covered up to one-third of the earth's surface, including much of northeastern North America. Whenever air temperatures plummeted, ice sheets slowly crept southward, spreading over large areas. During warmer periods, however, the ice melted and the glaciers partially melted away. Then land was uncovered again. Glaciers advanced and retreated so many times during the Pleistocene that it is often called the Great Ice Age.

When the ice sheets grew, they trapped large quantities of water. As a result, the earth's oceans shrank, sea levels fell, and coastal plains expanded. In the area of the Chesapeake Bay, the coastal plain extended all the way south to Cape Henry and Cape Charles. The ancient Susquehanna River flowed across the plain, almost 200 miles (300 kilometers) farther south than it does today.

About 12,000 years ago, the ice sheets finally retreated to the far north, and the melting waters began to flow into the earth's oceans. As sea levels gradually rose, the deep river valley that the Susquehanna River had cut into the plain slowly flooded. Eventually, the coastal plain was flooded too, forming the Chesapeake Bay. The bay reached its present size about 3,000 years ago.

Although many large rivers now carry freshwater to the Chesapeake Bay estuary, the Susquehanna is the largest.

AT ONE TIME, THE SUSQUEHANNA RIVER FOLLOWED A DIFFERENT COURSE. IT FLOWED FARTHER SOUTH ACROSS THE COASTAL PLAIN AND EMPTIED INTO THE ATLANTIC OCEAN.

About 50 percent of the freshwater that flows into Chesapeake Bay comes from the Susquehanna River.

As the Susquehanna meanders around Pennsylvania's mountains and hills, its shallow, fast-moving freshwater provides a home for many species of aquatic life. Fishes swim in the water, while mammals and amphibians make their homes along the river's banks. Waterfowl feed, breed, and raise their young in the trees and marshy areas that border the river channel. Microscopic organisms living in the water and in the soil serve as important food sources for the animals that live in or near the river.

The trip from the Susquehanna's headwaters in New York to its mouth at Havre de Grace, Maryland, is a 444-mile (715-kilometer) journey. As the freshwater moves closer and closer to Havre de Grace, it encounters and mixes with salt water that has been carried upstream by the rising ocean tide. This is where the Susquehanna River ends and the Chesapeake Bay estuary begins.

THE CHESAPEAKE BAY WATERSHED

There are more than 850 estuaries along the coastlines of the United States. The Chesapeake Bay is the largest. The bay itself is close to 200 miles (300 kilometer) long. It extends from the northeastern corner of Maryland southward to the capes that jut out into the Atlantic Ocean near Norfolk, Virginia. The width of the bay varies from 4 to 40 miles (6 to 60 kilometers).

Despite its tremendous size, Chesapeake Bay is a relatively shallow body of water. Although the water is more than 60 feet (20 meters) deep in some areas, the average water depth is about 20 feet (6 meters). The shoulders of the bay and its tributaries are usually less than 30 feet (9 meters) deep.

The area that supplies water to a body of water is called a watershed. Although Chesapeake Bay itself lies within the boundaries of Virginia and Maryland, its watershed extends over a much larger area. Water from land in New York, Pennsylvania, West Virginia, the District of Columbia, and Delaware ultimately drains into the bay. While the surface area of the bay is about 3,900 square miles (10,000 square kilometers), the area of its watershed is 64,000 square miles (170,000 square kilometers).

Rain and snow that fall in the Appalachian Mountains and other areas far from Chesapeake Bay supply the watershed with water. Much of the rain and melting snow soak into the ground. There, it becomes groundwater—water that flows through and around soil and rock beneath the land's surface. Some of the groundwater flows into the watershed's lakes, ponds, rivers, and streams. So does runoff—water that hasn't sunk into the ground. By flowing from creek to stream to river, the water eventually drains from the watershed into Chesapeake Bay.

Nineteen major rivers flow into the bay. Besides the mighty Susquehanna, large amounts of water come from the James, Potomac, Rappahannock, Patuxent, and Choptank Rivers. More than four hundred smaller rivers, streams, and creeks also flow into the bay. Each of these tributaries begins to form a separate estuary at some point upstream from the bay itself.

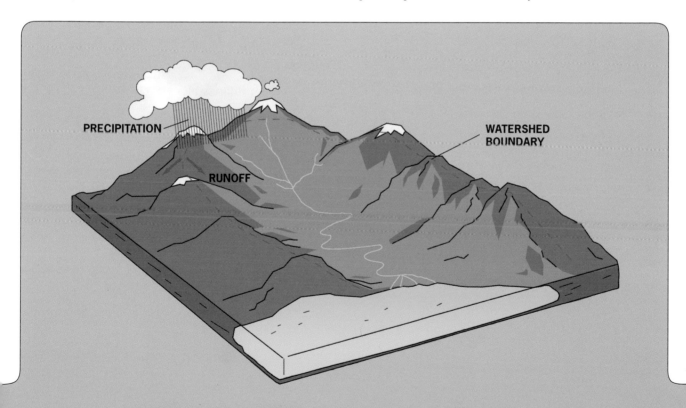

PRECIPITATION
RUNOFF
WATERSHED BOUNDARY

A WATERSHED IS THE AREA THAT SUPPLIES WATER TO A PARTICULAR BODY OF WATER.

Because the mixing of fresh and salt water occurs in so many places, all the water in the small upstream estuaries and in the bay is usually considered one big, interconnected estuary ecosystem. Think of the estuary as shaped like a giant glove with many fingers.

A CHANGING ECOSYSTEM

Chesapeake Bay is a dynamic estuary. It changes from season to season, day to day, and sometimes even hour to hour. Climate and weather affect the estuary's condition. If a summer is hot and little rain falls, the amount of water in the rivers and streams that feed Chesapeake Bay is reduced. Marshy areas may dry up completely, making it impossible for some creatures to survive. On the other hand, a season with extreme falls of rain or snow may result in floods that kill organisms that cannot live in water.

While weather conditions may occasionally cause unusual drying and flooding in the estuary, ocean tides bring about daily fluctuations in the estuary's water level. Organisms living in parts of the estuary that are subject to tidal changes must be able to endure both wet and dry periods.

The bay's water temperature varies from season to season. The water temperature may dip as low as 32° Fahrenheit (0° Celsius) in the winter and spike as high as 84° Fahrenheit (29° Celsius) in the summer. Air temperature also varies from season to season. Summertime temperatures easily soar to 90° Fahrenheit (32° Celsius) and above, while dropping to below freezing in the winter. Some organisms can tolerate the widely ranging temperatures, others can't. Those that can't migrate to other places until the temperature range suits them again.

The Chesapeake Bay ecosystem has another physical condition even more stressful to its organisms than climate, temperature, and water level changes. Salinity—the amount of salt present in the water, the soil, and even the air—often determines which organisms live in different parts of the estuary. For example, a bullfrog that lives in a freshwater marsh near the head of Chesapeake Bay cannot survive on a salty beach farther down the Bay near the ocean. Most organisms do not

SALT MARSH CORDGRASS (*SPARTINA ALTERNIFLORA*) IS A HARDY PLANT THAT HAS ADAPTED TO THE SALTY ESTUARY WATERS.

find it easy to adjust to changes in salinity.

Scientists divide estuaries into three broad zones based on the amount of salt present. The least salty water is found in the oligohaline zone. Water containing medium levels of salt belongs to the mesohaline zone. This zone includes the many salt marshes that fringe an estuary's shoreline. The land in salt marshes regularly floods and dries out as the tide flows in and out. Sometimes the soil and water are very salty, other times they are less so. The estuary's saltiest water is in the polyhaline zone, which in some places may be as salty as ocean water. The organisms found in this part of the estuary have developed bodies, leaves, or shelters that can deal with high concentrations of salt.

Wherever freshwater and salt water mix, many different kinds of chemical reactions occur. Many of these reactions create new chemical compounds. In some cases, the new materials dissolve in water. In other cases, the new materials precipitate, or solidify and fall to the bottom of the bay. Like salinity, these reactions affect the life and overall health of the estuary ecosystem.

Each of the freshwater rivers, streams, and creeks that discharges, or empties, into Chesapeake Bay also contributes in some way to the health of the estuary. So do the estuary's animals, plants, and other organisms. Together, the physical and living parts of the Chesapeake Bay estuary form a vital, important ecosystem.

CHAPTER 2
WHERE FRESHWATER AND SALT WATER MEET

High atop Butte Mountain in West Virginia, a snowflake falls on a pebble near a splashing, gurgling stream. The flake melts and the drop of water rolls off the pebble and lands in the stream with a soft plop. A creek in central New York zigzags across a grassy meadow and joins with another creek. Their waters mix and continue flowing toward the Pennsylvania border. In Pennsylvania, water in the mighty Susquehanna swirls around boulders in the riverbed. It detours around a mountain, and then continues its southerly journey. Water in the wide Potomac River drifts past Mount Vernon. Although they are separated by hundreds of miles, the stream, the creeks, and the two rivers have two things in common. They're all freshwater, and they're all draining toward Chesapeake Bay.

FRESHWATER IS MORE THAN H$_2$O

Depending on the kinds of rock and soil that freshwater flows through, it may contain many different substances. Pure freshwater is composed of two elements—hydrogen and oxygen. Water forms when two atoms of hydrogen combine with one atom of oxygen. The chemical formula for water is H$_2$O. But a number of other elements are commonly found in freshwater. Water dissolves these elements from the rock and soil it flows around and through. Elements and chemical compounds commonly found in river water include nitrogen, phosphorus, calcium, silicon, and iron.

Think about the rivers and streams you have seen. Was the water crystal clear or did it look a little brownish? That color comes from sediment—bits and pieces of rock, soil, and organic matter—swept up and transported by water currents. The turbidity, or cloudiness, of a river or stream depends on how much sediment is suspended in the water. Fast-moving water is generally more turbid than slow-moving water because sediment doesn't have time to settle to the bottom.

FROM RIVER TO ESTUARY

As the freshwater of the Susquehanna, the Potomac, and other large and small waterways approaches Chesapeake Bay, it begins to change. Twice a day, the Atlantic Ocean's tide cycle pushes salt water from the bay up into the mouths of the waterways. When the tide flows back out, salinity decreases as the flow of freshwater from the streams and rivers reasserts its dominance. At the place where the freshwater encounters the first salty water, the river ecosystem ends and the estuary ecosystem begins.

The salt in estuary water is very similar to the salt you sprinkle on French fries. It consists mostly of sodium chloride, which is made of the elements sodium and chlorine. While sodium chloride is also the most abundant salt in the ocean water just beyond the bay, seawater may also contain small amounts of up to fifty-three other salts.

Scientists determine how salty water is by measuring its salinity in parts per thousand (ppt)—the number of grams of dissolved salts in 1,000 grams of water. While the salinity of freshwater is usually less than 0.5 ppt, ocean water averages 30 to 35 ppt. The water in an estuary ecosystem falls somewhere in between.

FAST-MOVING WATER OFTEN APPEARS BROWN OR GREEN DUE TO THE AMOUNT OF SEDIMENT SUSPENDED IN IT.

THE OLIGOHALINE ZONE

As you learned earlier, an estuary can be divided into three zones according to the salinity of its water. The oligohaline zone is the least salty region of an estuary. Its salinity ranges from 0.5 to 5 ppt. In the Chesapeake Bay estuary, the oligohaline zone is found in tributaries, not in the open area of the bay. How far upstream the oligohaline zone extends varies from river to river and also changes with the seasons.

During the winter, snow and ice accumulate in the mountains and other cold regions. In spring, meltwater from the snow and ice sinks into the ground or runs off the land and into the streams and rivers. The additional water from melted snow and spring rains temporarily increases the amount of freshwater that enters the estuary. It also affects the force with which the water flows. The increase in the amount of freshwater dilutes the salinity, while the force of the current pushes the mixing zone farther downstream. Sometimes the force of the river current may be so great that it actually overpowers the force of the incoming tide's upstream movement. The Susquehanna River can sometimes overpower the bay's incoming tide for days at a time.

In summer and autumn, when conditions on the land are drier, less freshwater flows into the estuary. Then, the ocean tides force salt water farther up into the rivers, and the salinity in the oligohaline zone rises.

Currents in the oligohaline zone often churn sediment from the bottom of the estuary. The sediment

> BECAUSE SALT WATER IS DENSER, OR HEAVIER, THAN FRESHWATER, THE DEEPER WATER IN AN ESTUARY IS ALWAYS SALTIER THAN THE SURFACE WATERS.

swirls up and mixes with new sediment from the river. As a result, most of the turbid water in an estuary occurs in the oligohaline zone.

The salt water in this zone often circulates in a very interesting way. Because salt water is denser, or heavier, than freshwater, the deeper water in an estuary is always saltier than the surface waters. At some point, however, water circulation prevents salinity from increasing any further, so the bottom of the estuary isn't a layer of pure salt. As the salt water flows toward the riverbed, it forms a wedge-shaped layer. The narrow edge of the saltwater wedge points upstream, while the wider edge faces the salty sea. Meanwhile, the lighter freshwater flows over the heavier salt water.

Water currents, wind, and changes in temperature cause the two layers to mix. The result of this mixing is brackish, or slightly salty, water. While swift currents and mixing water can make living conditions harsh, they also keep a steady exchange of oxygen and nutrient-rich water moving between the surface and the bottom.

A SAND-RIMMED MARSH MAKES UP A PORTION OF THE CHESAPEAKE BAY SHORELINE.

Scientists often use the term water column when they discuss how well or poorly water in a certain area has mixed. The term defines a specific way of looking at an area of water. Imagine sticking a drinking straw straight down into a glass of water. The water inside the straw is a column of water that includes water from the surface all the way down to the bottom of the glass. Like the water enclosed by the straw, the water column is a core of water from a bay or river that includes water from the surface all the way down to the bottom.

The force of the ocean tide can determine how quickly and thoroughly layers of freshwater and salt water in the water column mix. If the force of the tide is about the same or slightly greater than the force of a river's flow, the two layers remain fairly distinct. If the ocean tide is stronger than a river's flow, however, the water layers are so quickly and thoroughly mixed that the salinity is equal from top to bottom of the water column.

Salinity in certain areas of the Chesapeake Bay also varies from side to side. In other words, the salinity on one side of the estuary is often greater than on the other side. Scientists believe that the Coriolis effect may be responsible. Named after French engineer Gaspard Coriolis, the Coriolis effect describes the influence the earth's rotation has on objects on our planet's surface. When an object in the Northern Hemisphere moves, it tends to deflect, or turn, toward the right. In the Southern Hemisphere, an object deflects toward the left.

In the Northern Hemisphere, the Coriolis effect deflects freshwater flowing seaward toward the right-hand shore (as you stand inland facing the ocean). The saltier water stays closer to the left-hand shore. That may be part of the reason water close to the Chesapeake Bay's eastern shore is saltier than water close to the western shore. (If you face seaward at the mouth of the Susquehanna River, the eastern shore would be on your left.) The eastern shore may also be saltier because there are fewer large rivers flowing into the bay along this shoreline.

It would be very tidy if all of the

freshwater and salt water mixing patterns and the way they influence salinity could be attributed to one cause. However, estuaries are not tidy ecosystems. They are always changing—that's what makes them challenging places for plants and animals to live. In reality, all the mixing patterns discussed so far can, and sometimes do, occur simultaneously in different parts of the estuary.

LIFE IN THE OLIGOHALINE ZONE

When water circulates within a water column, food moves downward and becomes available to benthic creatures—bottom-dwelling animals and microorganisms that live on or in the sediment. Because the Chesapeake Bay estuary is fairly shallow, its bottom dwellers, such as oysters, clams, worms, and sea stars, are well nourished.

At the same time, the benthic community bustles with activity as its members use physical and chemical processes to transform and recycle nutrients into energy. The energy moves back up the water column to nektonic creatures, such as herring, sharks, dolphins, and sea jellies, that freely swim through the estuary's surface waters. This exchange of energy and nutrients is one reason the Chesapeake Bay ecosystem is so productive, or rich with life. The organic (living) matter and inorganic (non-living) nutrients processed and produced by the bay's benthic organisms create a

A SWARM OF SEA NETTLES (CHRYSAORA FUSCESCENS), A TYPE OF SEA JELLY

REDHEAD GRASS *(POTAMOGETON PERFOLIATUS)*

WILD CELERY *(APIUM GRAVEOLENS)*

storehouse of food that is like a supermarket with overflowing shelves.

If you compare the diversity, or variety, of benthic organisms in an estuary with the diversity of those found in either a river or the ocean, you will find fewer species in the estuary. However, the benthic species that do live in estuaries are usually found in very large quantities because so much food is available for them to eat.

Some of the smaller plants that thrive in freshwater are able to survive in the oligohaline zone. Examples include redhead grass, waterweed, and wild celery. Redhead grass is easy to identify. It has heart-shaped leaves, a slender stem, and flowers that grow in a dense cluster. Waterweed, which features many-branched stems and dark green leaves, is often used in home aquariums. Wild celery grows in muddy, swirling water and looks nothing like the celery you buy in supermarkets. Its long, flat, ribbonlike leaves withstand swift water currents by bending and swaying. When water currents slow, wild celery resumes an upright position.

High-tide bush, a shrub that grows anywhere from 2 to 12 feet (0.6 to 3.7 meters) tall, also favors brackish water. Stands of saltgrass, common reed, and river bulrush are commonly found in brackish marshes that fringe the Chesapeake Bay.

Marsh periwinkles thrive in slightly salty water. These little, dark-colored snails are often spotted as they feed on blades of marsh grasses. They must remain moist at all times, so they never stray far from the water. Mussels, oval-shaped shellfish usually seen in clusters clinging to submerged rocks, also have no problem living in brackish water.

Canada geese are the most abundant waterfowl in the Chesapeake Bay area—even though overhunting has reduced their numbers in recent years. Scientists also believe that their reproduction rate is decreasing. Ducks are the second most abundant kind of waterfowl in the bay. Canvasbacks, mallards, black ducks, and

HOODED MERGANSER
(LOPHODYTES CUCULLATUS)

CANADA GOOSE
(BRANTA CANADENSIS)

mergansers are some of the species that spend time here.

Mammals such as raccoons, foxes, and otters live and hunt in areas where the water has become slightly salty. Shorebirds flock to the area, where they can feast on worms that burrow in the mud, snails that creep and crawl on plants, and small fishes that swim in the water. Even though some of the species that live in the freshwater upstream cannot survive close to the bay, the brackish waters of the oligohaline zone are a vibrant ecosystem that is an important part of the Chesapeake Bay estuary.

A RACCOON (*PROCYON LOTOR*) FORAGES FOR FOOD ON THE BANKS OF THE CHESAPEAKE BAY.

CHAPTER 3
THE WATER GETS MORE SALTY

As the water flows closer to the bay, its salinity gradually increases. Eventually, the brackish oligohaline zone merges into the more salty mesohaline zone. The mesohaline zone has a salinity of about 5 to 18 ppt. There is no well-defined line that separates the oligohaline zone from the mesohaline zone. The boundaries of the zones are blurred and change with the seasons and with the tides.

If you hop into a boat and sail toward a shoreline area that is usually part of Chesapeake Bay's mesohaline zone, you might see all kinds of fishes darting beneath the boat and plants growing on the bottom. As the boat moves closer to shore, you begin to see grassy plants poking up out of the water. Soon the grasses grow so closely together that the area seems like a dry meadow. But don't jump out of the boat—unless you're wearing waders! Most of the ground is waterlogged and you might sink into the mud.

The tangled roots of the grasses and other plants that grow here are thick and closely interwoven. The soil quickly soaks up the salty water and holds it like a sponge. You are in a salt marsh, one of the most productive areas of the estuary. Most of the Chesapeake Bay's salt marshes fringe its eastern shore, opposite the mouths of the Potomac and Patuxent Rivers.

> MOST OF THE CHESAPEAKE BAY'S SALT MARSHES FRINGE ITS EASTERN SHORE, OPPOSITE THE MOUTHS OF THE POTOMAC AND PATUXENT RIVERS.

A wide range of salinity may be found within salt marsh areas. In some areas the salinity may even dip into the range of the oligohaline zone. However, most of the salt marshes along the edges of the Chesapeake Bay estuary are close to the open areas of the bay, where salinity levels are higher, even in the sand and mud. For this reason, salt marshes will be considered within this book as part of the mesohaline zone.

LIFE IN A SALT MARSH

Life is a real challenge for organisms in a salt marsh. Ocean tides flood the low areas of the salt marsh with salty water twice a day. Then, the plants, animals, and other organisms must be able to survive underwater. During low tide, the water recedes and the higher areas of the salt marsh are left completely exposed to the air. Then, the organisms must be able to survive drying out.

Some of the plants and animals that live in the salt marshes along the edges of the Chesapeake Bay estuary have developed special body structures that make it easier to live in a salty place with alternating wet and dry periods and swift water currents. The thick, waxy leaves of spatterdock and salt marsh aster help these plants combat salty conditions, tidal wetting and drying, and windy breezes. The waxy protection prevents water from evaporating from the plant.

Cordgrasses dominate all the salt marshes surrounding Chesapeake Bay. This hardy group of plants cannot live outside the mesohaline zone. They need salt. Some members of this group have glands in their long, slender leaves and stems that pump

SALT MEADOW CORDGRASS (SPARTINA PATENS) CAN GROW TO BE 3 FEET (0.9 METER) TALL.

out salt. If you look closely at these plants, you can see discarded salt crystals on their leaves. If you licked a blade of cordgrass, you would be able to taste the salt.

Salt marsh cordgrass, which may grow more than 5 feet (2 meters) tall, prefers areas where tidal currents are strong. Its leaves can tolerate being submerged for fairly long periods of time. The plant's rhizomes—horizontal stems that lie along or just beneath the soil—anchor the cordgrass firmly in place and store food for the growing plant.

When salt marsh cordgrass dies or blades of the grass are broken off, the receding tide picks them up and carries the plants—and the bacteria and algae that live on them—into the open water of the estuary. As a result, the cordgrass is an important source of food for a variety of creatures in the mesohaline zone.

One of these cordgrass-eating creatures is the marsh snail, which spends its days sliding up and down the plant's blades. Along the way, the snail nibbles on the algae growing on the cordgrass. Marsh snails don't require an enormous amount of living space. In some salt marshes, as many as two thousand have been counted in a 3.3-square-foot (0.31 square meter) area.

Salt meadow cordgrass, yet another member of the cordgrass family, also grows in salt marshes—but at a slightly higher elevation. The land this 1- to 3-foot-tall (0.3- to 0.9-meter-tall), purplish plant grows on is not regularly flooded by tides.

All the cordgrasses are constantly being eaten by bacteria and fungi. These tiny creatures break down the cellulose—the

MARSH SNAILS (*LITTORINA IRRORATA*) CLINGING TO SALT MARSH CORDGRASS

woody plant material—found in the cordgrasses' stems and leaves and convert it into energy. When the bacteria and fungi die or are gobbled up by other creatures, that energy continues its journey through the estuary's food chain.

Meanwhile, clusters of mussels spend their days clinging to the horizontal roots of cordgrass plants. They feed by siphoning water in and out of their bodies. Some mussels release phosphorus into the water. This nutrient helps the cordgrass grow. Scientists have discovered that when the mussels are removed from a bed of cordgrass, the plants don't grow as well.

How do mussels survive being left high and dry by receding tides? They protect their soft, moist bodies by keeping their shells tightly closed. The moisture inside the shell is enough to sustain them until the tide turns and water floods the area again.

Fiddler crabs burrow in and around the cordgrass. Their holes help the soil drain and let oxygen flow down to the plants' roots. The increase in oxygen speeds the decay process, which contributes to detritus—the little bits and pieces of organic material, soil, and sand found on the bottom. Detritus is

MUSSELS
(ANODONTA)

FIDDLER CRAB
(UCA MINAX)

an important source of food for many of the small animals in the estuary.

Amphipods—tiny shrimplike creatures—are common in estuaries all over the world. Beach fleas and beach hoppers are the amphipods you are likely to encounter on the mesohaline zone's beaches and in salt marshes. They often live under piles of dead or drying seaweed. If you lift the seaweed, they usually hop high into the air.

Many of the larger animals found in the Chesapeake Bay's salt marshes are "commuters." They visit the area to eat or spend a short part of their life and then move on to another area of the bay. The white-tailed deer is one of the large mammals that can be found in salt marshes. To stay healthy, deer need salt in their diet, and a salt marsh is an ideal place to get it. Beavers, raccoons, muskrats, and otters often venture into salt marshes as they hunt for food. Several species of rats and mice nest in cordgrasses and other salt marsh vegetation.

Waterfowl are also abundant in and around Chesapeake Bay's salt marshes. Many geese, ducks, and other migratory birds stop over at the estuary. At certain

BEACH FLEA
(TALORCHESTIA MEGALOPTHALMA)

RIVER OTTER
(LUTRA CANADENSIS)

times of the year, the sky above the Chesapeake Bay estuary teems with birds. More than one million birds use the Atlantic flyway over the bay every year.

Chesapeake Bay is also the winter habitat for a large number of birds. Each autumn, tundra swans leave their summertime homes in the northernmost reaches of North America and spend the winter in the Chesapeake Bay estuary. Twenty-nine other species of waterfowl use the bay as their winter home, breeding ground, or temporary rest stop.

Sandpipers wade in the shallow water hunting for small fishes and worms. Shorebirds such as seagulls, terns, sandpipers, rails, herons, and egrets nest and raise families in the marsh grasses year-round. Hawks and ospreys also hunt and nest in the area. In fact, the nation's largest population of ospreys is in the Chesapeake Bay region. These large, fish-eating birds nest in trees near salt marshes, so they can be close to the water and their next meal.

IN THE MESOHALINE'S WATERS

Just beyond the edge of a salt marsh, the shallow water of the mesohaline zone thrives with life. There are worms with special coverings to limit the amount of salt water that passes into their bodies. These creatures wriggle through the bottom sediment in search of nutrients.

You'll also find plenty of fishes in the salty water. Some have a slimy coating on their skin that minimizes the amount of salt their bodies absorb.

TUNDRA SWANS *(OLOR COLUMBIANUS)* PAD ACROSS THE ICE.

SECONDARY CONSUMER: A LOOK AT OSPREYS

The osprey, one of the Chesapeake Bay's most important secondary consumers, is usually found close to water. Ospreys are raptors—birds that hunt and kill prey. The bay area is a good place for ospreys because fish and marine animals, their preferred meals, are in plentiful supply.

The osprey is one of the largest raptors in the estuary. A full-grown adult may have a wingspan of up to 67 inches (170 centimeters). The osprey carries its powerful wings in a high, arched position during flight, enabling the bird to lift a fish weighing as much as 4 pounds (2 kilograms) and carry it to shore. At that weight, the fish may be heavier than the osprey. By keeping its wings arched, the osprey avoids dipping them into the water. If the bird's wings became waterlogged, it would be too heavy to fly.

When an osprey's keen, yellow eyes spot a fish, the bird first hovers and then tucks its wings close to its body. The bird plummets toward the water, its legs extended. Its sharp talons slice into the water and close around the fish. Special pads on the underside of the osprey's toes are covered with little spines, called spicules, that help the bird grab a slippery fish tightly.

Ospreys make their nests out of sticks. The nests are built at the tops of trees, on cliff ledges, or even on top of telephone or electrical power line poles. The female lays two to four whitish eggs that are spotted with reddish-brown splotches. While the female tends the eggs, the male brings her food.

When use of the pesticide DDT was permitted in the United States, osprey populations dropped drastically in number and the bird's survival was considered threatened. Since the pesticide was banned in 1972, the number of ospreys has slowly risen.

Fishes and other nektonic organisms have yet another way of coping with salinity. If the water they're in is too salty, they simply swim away. Most of the time, these creatures move up and down the estuary, more or less traveling with the tides.

In winter, fishes living in a shallow estuary or bay such as the Chesapeake have a special problem: the salt water can get colder than the temperature at which most fish blood freezes. The winter flounder has a trick for dealing with this problem. It has developed a way to alter its blood chemistry slightly in order to lower the temperature at which its blood freezes. By using this trick and staying in the estuary's deep water, the winter flounder is able to survive.

Many fishes spawn in the mesohaline zone. These fish species have developed ways to cope with the estuary's swift water currents. Some lay eggs that stick to rocks and plants, so they won't be swept away. To deal with the estuary's alternating dry and wet conditions, silversides lay eggs with an unusual outer covering that will not dry out if the eggs are exposed to the sun when the tide flows out.

Shrimp, crayfish, crabs, and clams all live on the estuary's tidal flats—areas left exposed when the tide is low. These hard-shelled animals spend most of their time hunting and feeding. Some species of crabs roll mud into pellets when the tide goes out. When the tide flows back in, the crabs quickly scurry into their burrows and plug

MANTIS SHRIMP (*ODONTODACTYLUS SCYLLARUS*)

the opening with the mud pellets.

Soft-shelled clams are most common in places where the water is less than 20 feet (6 meters) deep at high tide. Although these clams normally inhabit the mesohaline zone, they sometimes move upriver to water where the salinity may be as low as 5 ppt. Like mussels and oysters, clams close their shells when the tide goes out and when the salt level doesn't suit them. They may also burrow down into the sand or mud.

Animals are not the only organisms you'll find living in the mesohaline's watery world. More than fifty species of submerged aquatic vegetation (SAV)—plants that grow below the water's surface—grow in the world's estuaries. About thirteen of these plants are found in Chesapeake Bay. Which plants grow where is determined by salinity, water depth, and the kind of sediment on the bottom.

The two most common kinds of SAV in the Chesapeake Bay's mesohaline zone are eelgrass and widgeon grass. The flat, narrow leaves of eelgrass resemble long green ribbons. This plant usually grows in sandy mud. Widgeon grass, which has

EELGRASS (*ZOSTERA MARINA*) HELPS TO INCREASE WATER CLARITY AND REDUCE EROSION BY REDUCING WAVE ENERGY AND TRAPPING LOOSE SEDIMENT.

thin, branching leaves, spreads into river mouths and farther upstream than eelgrass because it can tolerate a wider range of salinities.

Submerged aquatic vegetation sways with the water currents the way grasses on land sway and bend on a breezy day. Water currents often erode, or wash away, the sand and mud they flow over, but waving stands of SAV can reduce the currents and limit shoreline erosion. SAV also filters out sediment suspended in the water. Sediment trapped by plant leaves and stems is less likely to settle to the bottom and bury the creatures living there. Some bottom dwellers, such as oysters, will suffocate if sediment piles too deeply on top of them.

In addition, SAV stems and leaves provide food and shelter for fishes, birds, shellfish, and the many small creatures that crawl about or burrow in the bottom. When many of the hard-shelled creatures in Chesapeake Bay molt, or shed their hard outer coverings as part of their growth process, they hide among SAV while they wait for their new shells to harden. The plants help keep the animals safe from hungry predators.

The mesohaline zone's increased salinity levels don't harm the estuary ecosystem at all. By adapting to the mesohaline's challenging demands, many organisms flourish and survive in large numbers. Their presence makes important contributions to the estuary's productivity.

CHAPTER 4
THE ESTUARY'S SALTIEST WATER

If you board a boat in Baltimore, Maryland, and sail down Chesapeake Bay to the Atlantic Ocean, you would begin your journey in the bay's oligohaline zone. After traveling south for about 30 miles (50 kilometers), you would be floating into the mesohaline zone, where the salinity is higher. If it were spring, you might remain in the mesohaline zone all the way down the bay until your boat sailed near the mouth of the York River, within sight of the bay's mouth. If it were autumn, however, the mesohaline zone might end as far north as the mouth of the Potomac River.

Regardless of your actual position, when you sail into the estuary's saltiest water, you leave the mesohaline zone behind and enter the polyhaline zone. The polyhaline zone has a salinity of about 18 to 30 ppt.

Although the polyhaline zone is most often found very close to the mouth of the bay, it's important to remember that its border is not fixed in one area. Depending on the time of year, the amount of rainfall, and water currents from the ocean, the blurry boundaries of the polyhaline zone move up and down the bay—and even into the mouths of some of the tributaries. Salinity levels between 18 and 21 ppt are common several miles up the James, York, Pocomoke, and Rappahannock Rivers.

THE POTOMAC RIVER IS ONE OF THE NINETEEN MAJOR RIVERS THAT FLOW INTO CHESAPEAKE BAY.

MICROORGANISMS IN THE POLYHALINE ZONE

Chesapeake Bay's polyhaline zone teems with plankton—microscopic free-floating organisms that live in water. The abundance of each plankton species varies according to the season. For the most part, one species dominates during a particular time of year. Sunny days, favorable temperatures, and a good supply of nutrients encourage photoplankton, such as algae, diatoms, and dinoflagellates, to reproduce. As these tiny organisms multiply, they attract a variety of primary consumers. Wherever primary consumers congregate, secondary consumers soon arrive.

If you were to fill a dishpan with estuary water and look at it closely, you might see a dozen or so tiny creatures floating and swimming around. If you looked at the same water under a microscope, you would see lots more. These small animals, found in the waters of all estuaries, are called zooplankton. An average-sized bathtub filled with water from Chesapeake Bay would contain more than three million of these tiny creatures. Unlike photoplankton, zooplankton are not primary producers. Depending on the species, they may be either primary or secondary consumers.

Zooplankton are an important link in an estuary ecosystem's food chain. The larvae, or very young forms, of many fishes and other bay creatures eat zooplankton. Energy continues its journey up the ecosystem's food chain when the larvae are gobbled up by larger fishes, birds, and other wildlife.

> IF YOU WERE TO FILL A DISHPAN WITH ESTUARY WATER AND LOOK AT IT CLOSELY, YOU MIGHT SEE A DOZEN TINY CREATURES SWIMMING AROUND.
> IF YOU LOOKED AT THE SAME WATER UNDER A MICROSCOPE, YOU WOULD SEE LOTS MORE.

Zooplankton are not strong swimmers, so they are usually carried up and down in the bay and in the water column by water currents. As zooplankton drift along, they search for food. Most of the time, they dine on algae.

Zooplankton are divided into two broad categories. Holoplankton spend their entire lives as members of the zooplankton. Meroplankton are larvae that eventually develop into adult snails, oysters, crabs, fishes, shrimp, worms, or sea jellies.

Copepods are the most widespread and abundant kind of holoplankton. More than thirty species of copepods live in Chesapeake Bay, but just five kinds account for 95 percent of the copepods living in the bay at any given time. Copepods thrive in very salty water, but they can live in freshwater too. These hardy creatures can also withstand a wide range of water temperatures.

Copepods consume a variety of foods, including algae, bacteria, decomposing marsh grasses, and other bits of plant material. How do they find their prey? Copepods are filter feeders. They draw water into their bodies and strain their food from it. Copepods filter as much as 1 quart (1 liter) of water a day, removing the nutrients they need to survive. Meroplankton often feed on copepods, so a healthy copepod population is critical for sustaining an estuary ecosystem.

Water fleas are another important kind of zooplankton. These microscopic

CRAB ZOEAE (LARVAE) ARE A KIND OF ZOOPLANKTON.

polyhaline dwellers look like a cross between a shrimp and a flea. In spring and summer, water fleas are an important food source for fish, but during autumn and winter, their population shrinks by 50 percent. Then the fish must find other things to eat.

BENTHIC ANIMALS IN THE POLYHALINE ZONE

Animal life in the polyhaline zone is very diverse. In addition to the larvae and lifelong microorganisms that make up zooplankton, there is a variety of larger animals. Many species of benthic dwellers inhabit the tidal flats and the shallow waters in the lower part of Chesapeake Bay. While milky ribbon worms, limy tubeworms, and mantis shrimp tunnel through the bottom sediment, other creatures scurry about the top of the sediment.

Mole crabs live on sandy beaches near the mouth of the bay, close to the waves' breaking edges. When a wave's energy is spent and it begins "running" back toward the water, tiny mole crabs left exposed by the retreating water quickly burrow into the sand. These harmless, light gray crabs have no pinchers.

In sheltered areas where water currents are slow, very fine particles of sediment settle to the bottom. Nassa mud snails and five species of mud crabs feed on these small particles. The 1.5-inch-long (3.8-centimeter-long) common black-fingered mud crab is the largest of the

MOST CRABS WALK SIDEWAYS, BUT THE MOLE CRAB (EMERITA TALPOIDA) ALWAYS MOVES BACKWARD.

mud crabs. Mud crabs can tolerate the high salinity of the polyhaline zone, but they also thrive in the mesohaline zone.

Shellfish, such as knobbed whelks and hard clams called cherrystones, can also be found in the lower part of the bay. The clams burrow down into the sediment and extend their tubelike siphons up into the water. One of a clam's two siphons draws in oxygen and water containing food, the other expels waste material. Whelks extend their large feet and slide over the bottom. Meanwhile, sea stars and sea cucumbers use their tiny tube feet to alternately stick to and release objects as they creep from place to place.

Some benthic animals are sessile, which means they are not free to move around as adults. Sponges, oysters, mussels, sea anemones, sea squirts, and barnacles anchor themselves to rocks or other hard underwater surfaces as larvae. Because they can't leave their "spot," these creatures are at the mercy of predators and severe weather.

Barnacles are fascinating creatures. A barnacle's hard, cone-shaped home consists of six overlapping shell plates, a base

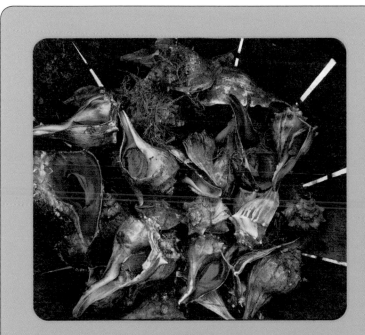

WHELKS (BUSYCOTYPUS CANALICULATUM)

COMMON BARNACLES (BALANUS GLANDULA)

WHAT OYSTERS CAN TELL US

In every ecosystem, certain plants and animals are considered indicator species. When an ecosystem is healthy, the population of an indicator species remains stable. By monitoring indicator species, scientists can determine the overall state of an ecosystem. If their population skyrockets or crashes, the entire ecosystem is probably out of balance.

One of the most important indicator species in the Chesapeake Bay estuary is the American oyster. This shellfish is most common in the shallow, salty waters of the polyhaline zone and in the tidal creeks and streams along the estuary's southern coastal shores.

Oysters are usually found on hard, rocky bottoms 8 to 25 feet (2 to 7.6 meters) below the water's surface. This is where the bay's warmest water is found. In summer, when the water throughout the bay warms up, each female oyster releases as many as one hundred thousand eggs, and males discharge billions of sperm. Only some of the eggs become fertilized and hatch into larvae, and many of those quickly become fish food. Oyster larvae spend their first 2 weeks of life drifting on water currents as meroplankton.

As their growing shells become heavier, the larvae fall to the bottom and seek a suitable anchor. An oyster larva's foot secretes a sticky substance that permanently glues it to hard sandy bottoms, rocks, or old oyster shells. Once the larva is attached, it is called a spat. Oysters never attach themselves to soft, loose sediment because as water currents shift the sediment they could be buried and suffocate. Only about one in ten thousand fertilized eggs survives to adulthood.

Like clams and mussels, oysters are filter feeders. As they suck water through their bodies, they remove plankton and other tiny creatures. Most of the time, oysters keep their shells open, but if the temperature, turbidity, or salinity changes unexpectedly, these shellfish snap their shells shut and wait for better times.

securely cemented to a hard surface, and two "doors" on top that the tiny animal inside can open and close. A barnacle can increase the size of its home by secreting new layers of calcium carbonate at the edges of the plates. When a barnacle is covered by water, it opens the doors of its home and extends a feathery looking fan of appendages. These appendages sway back and forth and sweep particles of food into the barnacle's mouth.

When barnacle eggs hatch, the tiny larvae become members of the meroplankton. Later, they find a suitable place to anchor themselves. Barnacles aren't picky about where they make their homes. They may attach themselves to rocks, aluminum cans, ropes, driftwood, or the bottom of a boat.

Benthic animals change the bottom of an estuary in several ways. They deposit feces, or waste matter, that forms a new layer of sediment. Some benthic animals, corals for example, change the bottom by building reefs. Oysters build oyster bars. Coral reefs and oyster bars grow as new animals anchor themselves and grow on top of old layers of shells. Most reefs and oyster bars do not break the water's surface.

NEKTONIC ANIMALS IN THE POLYHALINE ZONE

Many species of fishes can be found in the polyhaline zone of the Chesapeake Bay estuary, but sea jellies and worms are also important members of the nektonic community. So are aquatic mammals, such as dolphins.

Sea nettles, perhaps the best known sea jellies in Chesapeake Bay, dominate the high-salinity waters of the estuary. As they are carried along by water and wind currents, they occasionally contract their large umbrella-shaped bodies to point themselves in the desired direction. Long tentacles covered with stinging cells hang down from the sea nettle's body and sting any prey that happens to pass by. As soon as the victim is immobilized, the sea nettle eats it. Sea nettles often float in waters toward the head of the bay, but they die when the salinity is less than 5 ppt.

During the winter months, winter jellies are common throughout the estuary, while moon jellies are prevalent in the southern regions of the bay.

Sea walnuts belong to a group of animals known as the comb jellies. Although they resemble sea jellies, their internal body structure is different, and they don't have stinging cells. Sea walnuts spend most of their time zooming through the water in search of zooplankton. Because comb jellies are transparent and have no tentacles, it's often hard to see them during the day. But if a comb jelly is disturbed at night, its body glows a soft, light green color.

Schools of Chesapeake Bay herrings, such as menhaden and American shad, as well as anchovies swarm through the salty open waters of the estuary. These fishes can tolerate varying degrees of salinity and are not confined to the polyhaline zone. Fishes found only in the bay's saltiest waters include northern and southern kingfish, tautog, pigfish, and sheepshead.

Several species of stingrays and sharks frequent the bay's seagrass meadows. Cownose rays swim in shallow water. They propel themselves by gently waving their large pectoral fins, which look like

TAUTOG (*TAUTOGA ONITIS*)

wings. The largest animals have a 3-foot (1-meter) wingspan. As they glide along the bottom in search of prey, cownose rays periodically fan their wings to uncover soft-shell clams buried in the sediment. Schools of bluntnose stingrays often swim into the bay from the Atlantic Ocean.

Sandbar sharks are one of the estuary's top-level consumers. The young sharks spend much of their time in the bay's seagrass beds, searching for blue crabs and other tasty prey. During the summer, the youngsters swim in schools through the southern part of the bay. Adult sandbar sharks may reach 7 feet (2 meters) in length. Bull sharks and smooth dogfish are two other members of the shark family that regularly visit the bay.

All of the residents of the polyhaline zone—whether they are members of the benthic or nektonic communities—contribute to the estuary. Their presence is required to help maintain the ecosystem and a healthy balance among the estuary's three zones.

COWNOSE RAYS (RHINOPTERA BONASUS)

BLUE CRABS (CALINECTES SAPIDUS) ARE A FAVORITE FOOD OF MANY OF CHESAPEAKE BAY'S TOP-LEVEL CONSUMERS.

CHAPTER 5
MAINTAINING THE BALANCE

The Chesapeake Bay estuary is a complex and dynamic ecosystem. It has a diverse array of physical conditions. Salinity is in constant flux throughout the ecosystem. It is affected by seasonal changes, weather patterns, and water currents. Air and water temperatures change dramatically from summer to winter. The turbidity of the water ranges from crystal clear to murky and sediment filled.

The bay is also home to diverse populations of organisms—producers and consumers—that all play an important role in the ecosystem. The constant interaction between the organisms and the physical environment helps the ecosystem remain balanced and healthy. Plants and other primary producers supply oxygen and food to the system. Consumers receive energy by eating the producers or other consumers. Scavengers and decomposers clean up the remains of decaying plants and animals.

When each part of this diverse web—living or nonliving—functions normally, the ecosystem remains balanced. However, if any part of the ecosystem falters or is destroyed, the repercussions may be observed throughout the whole ecosystem. By now you are probably wondering what kinds of problems or stresses can

IF ANY PART OF THE ECOSYSTEM FALTERS OR IS DESTROYED, THE REPERCUSSIONS MAY BE OBSERVED THROUGHOUT THE WHOLE ECOSYSTEM.

disrupt the Chesapeake Bay estuary. In the next section, we will examine this question.

TOO MUCH OF A GOOD THING

Algae occupy a very important place in the estuary ecosystem. As primary producers, they are a critical food source for many consumers. Clumps of floating algae also provide a good hiding place for young lined seahorses and other small creatures. When algae are present in normal amounts, the ecosystem remains balanced and healthy. But when algae multiply too quickly, life throughout the ecosystem is affected.

When too much phosphorus and nitrogen find their way into the estuary, the growth rate of algae goes haywire. Algae thrive on these nutrients, and the population grows by leaps and bounds. The rapid growth causes the floating algae to form thick mats, called algal blooms, on the water's surface. As the algal mat thickens, the lower layers no longer receive enough sunlight to carry on photosynthesis. As a result, they die and begin to rot.

AN ALGAL BLOOM CAN UPSET AN AQUATIC ECOSYSTEM.

The decay process requires oxygen. When unusually large quantities of algae suddenly begin decaying, there is less oxygen available for animals to breathe. This upsets the entire ecosystem. If seahorses and other primary consumers die, what are secondary consumers supposed to eat? Soon their populations begin to decline too.

Submerged aquatic vegetation (SAV) growing beneath the algal mat also suffers. The mat prevents sunlight from reaching the SAV. Unable to carry on photosynthesis, the plants die.

Fortunately, other components—both nonliving and living—of the ecosystem interact with the algal bloom and work to restore balance. Swiftly flowing water, such as currents from a river swelled with rain or storm-driven ocean waves, carry oxygen to the depleted area. They also can break up the algal mats. Once SAV can grow again, it will add oxygen to the water and remove phosphorus and nitrogen. In time, the ecosystem will return to normal.

THE ROLE OF SAV

Submerged aquatic vegetation is an extremely important component of the estuary ecosystem. The roots of these plants keep bottom sediment stable and in one place. The leaves and stems provide food and shelter to many organisms. Snails and small fish graze on SAV. Worms, clams, and other burrowing creatures depend on nutrients released when

LINED SEAHORSES (*HIPPOCAMPUS ERECTUS*)

SAV dies and decays. Beds of SAV also serve as nursery areas—places where young fishes, such as menhaden and croakers, grow into adults.

To live and grow, SAV needs plenty of sunlight and nutrients. These plants cannot survive if the water's turbidity level rises too much and a lot of sediment remains suspended in the water column.

If a large amount of SAV dies, bottom dwelling organisms may have trouble finding food or shelter. Snails will starve. Young fish will be easily seen by hungry predators. If fewer fish survive to adulthood, the shorebirds that normally eat them will also have trouble surviving. Eventually, the mammals and reptiles that feed on shorebirds and their eggs will starve too.

SAV supplies the ecosystem with some of the oxygen it needs to remain balanced. Without SAV to add oxygen to the water column, many aquatic organisms would suffer.

SAV even helps reduce shoreline erosion. Without these plants, the Chesapeake Bay's water currents would race landward and scour the soil with their full force. In the process, animal homes would be destroyed and shoreline plants unable to withstand flooding would die.

SAV, algae, and oysters may not seem that important, but it's difficult to judge the importance of individual creatures in the Chesapeake Bay estuary. When the population of just one plant or animal species declines, the damage may ultimately extend throughout the entire ecosystem.

A SCHOOL OF ATLANTIC MENHADEN (BREVOORTIA TYRANNUS)

A PLACE FOR THE BIRDS

Like algae, SAV, and oysters, waterfowl and wading birds have an important role to play in the Chesapeake Bay estuary. They feed on SAV and other plants as well as snails, shrimp, mussels, clams, and small fish. As primary and secondary consumers, birds help control the populations of the species they eat. In addition, their waste matter returns precious nutrients to the ecosystem.

When the number of birds in the estuary suddenly declines, the effects quickly spread throughout the ecosystem. Populations of snails and small fishes explode, eating more than their fair share of SAV. As their food supplies diminish, many of the little creatures starve. For a while, there are very few snails and small fish in the estuary. SAV is also less plentiful than normal.

If the rest of the ecosystem is healthy, the populations of all these organisms gradually rebalance themselves. The small animals reproduce at a slower rate, and SAV beds regrow. As long as the bird population rebounds with the populations of snails and small fishes, a new equilibrium is eventually established.

WHEN ONE ZONE JUST ISN'T ENOUGH

Many estuary organisms spend their entire lives in the oligohaline zone, while others inhabit the mesohaline or the polyhaline instead. But most fishes need to move

THE LAUGHING GULL (LARUS ATRICILLA) IS ONE BIRD THAT HUNTS IN CHESAPEAKE BAY.

around. During some parts of the year, many may be found in the oligohaline zone, but a few months later they may have migrated elsewhere—perhaps out of the estuary and into the ocean. Except for a few species of fish, such as the small, minnowlike killifish, very few of the nearly three hundred fish species observed in the Chesapeake Bay estuary spend their entire lives there. Many of the part-time residents, such as the striped bass, are anadromous fish—they must move from ocean water to freshwater to spawn.

Striped bass—also called stripers or rockfish—are beautiful fish. They range in color from light green to almost black. They get their name from the stripes that run the length of their bodies. As these fish swim, rays of sunlight strike their sides and belly, flashing a brilliant, iridescent silver. A full-grown striped bass may reach nearly 5 feet (1.5 meters) in length and may weigh close to 100 pounds (45 kilograms).

Between April and June, adult stripers move from the salty, lower area of the bay to areas where the water is fresher. They swim into the larger rivers and creeks, stopping only when they reach the areas where salt water and freshwater first meet. When females find a spot with a strong water current, they lay their eggs. The eggs and larvae depend on the current to keep them suspended in the water column. If the eggs or larvae settle to the bottom, they will be covered with sediment and suffocate.

As young stripers grow, they slowly move downstream in search of SAV beds, where there is plenty of food and shelter.

STRIPED BASS (MORONE SAXATILIS)

BLUE CRABS HELP KEEP THE ESTUARY HEALTHY

Blue crabs live throughout the Chesapeake Bay estuary—from the oligohaline to the polyhaline zones. Males usually travel farther upstream, while females tend to remain in places where the water is saltier. The crabs spend their days scurrying across the bottom sediment in search of decomposing fish. By eating dead animals, blue crabs help keep the water clean. Blue crabs also eat plants, as well as living oysters and clams and even other blue crabs that have recently shed their hard shells.

Blue crabs—especially the larvae—are an important food source for other animals. The scientific name for the blue crab is *Callinectes sapidus*. Translated from its Greek and Latin roots, this name means "beautiful and tasty swimmer." The crab's common name, blue crab, comes from its bright blue to bluish green claws and shell.

A blue crab has ten jointed legs that are attached along the side and back edges of its body. The two front legs end in large pincers that are used to gather food and to defend the crab. Six spindly walking legs—three on each side—support the crab's body as it scuttles in and out of the vegetation growing on the bottom of the estuary. The two rear legs look like flat paddles and help the crab swim.

BLUE CRAB (*CALLINECTES SAPIDUS*)

Like lobsters, shrimp, and insects, a blue crab has a hard outer covering called an exoskeleton. As the crab grows, its exoskeleton becomes too tight. It occasionally splits open and the animal emerges surrounded by a new wrinkly, soft shell that is about one-third larger than the old one. Until the new shell hardens a few days later, the crab is a prime target for sandbar sharks and other predators.

Between May and October, blue crabs search for partners and mate. Then females spawn, or produce eggs, in the saltiest parts of the estuary or even in the open ocean. Each female lays a spongy, golden mass of up to two million fertilized eggs and attaches the eggs to the abdominal area of her shell. As the eggs develop, the spongy mass turns black.

After about a month, the eggs hatch and tiny larvae, called zoeae, swim out into the water. Zoeae do not look at all like adult crabs. After molting several times, they begin to migrate upward in the water column, and tidal currents sweep them toward less salty regions of the estuary.

After about 40 days, the zoeae molt a final time and become megalopae—the blue crab's second larval stage. Megalopae are almost twice the size of zoeae, but they are still tiny. As they crawl along the bottom—continuing to travel farther from the salty ocean—megalopae molt into recognizable blue crabs.

The young crabs molt several more times during the next 12 to 16 months. By then, they are about 5 inches (12 centimeters) across and ready to have young of their own. Adult crabs may grow to be up to 9 inches (23 centimeters) across. Of the two million eggs a female blue crab lays, an average of only two will reach adulthood.

In the winter, when the water temperature drops below 50° Fahrenheit (10° Celsius), blue crabs are dormant, or inactive. During this period, females are most likely to be found in the lower regions, or mouth, of the bay. Males remain in less salty water, where they burrow into the mud.

The young fish spend the summer feeding and growing in the shallow brackish water. Young stripers eagerly gobble copepods, water fleas, and insect larvae, keeping those populations in balance. The waste material produced by the juvenile stripers settles to the bottom of the estuary, where it adds nutrients to the sediment and provides energy for benthic feeders.

As long as the water temperature stays fairly constant, young stripers will thrive in the SAV environment—even though many will be devoured by larger fish, crabs, and birds. Although many stripers are eaten, their sacrifice is important to the ecosystem. They provide energy for secondary consumers. This keeps the oligohaline and mesohaline zones healthy. When secondary consumers eat striper eggs and larvae, they prevent the striper population from growing too large. That keeps the polyhaline zone healthy. If the adult striper population in the polyhaline zone were to grow too large, its food source would become depleted and the overall health of the zone would suffer.

While young stripers are busy growing in the mesohaline zone, the adults are spending the summer months feeding in the salty water along the shallow edges of the bay. As winter approaches and the water temperature drops, all stripers—adults and juveniles—move to deeper water at the center of the bay.

The life cycle of another common bay fish, the American eel, is the reverse of the striper's. Young eels hatch in the open ocean and then swim into the estuary, where they live for several years. When the eels are fully grown, they migrate to their

AMERICAN EELS (ANGUILLA ROSTRATA)

spawning grounds in the Atlantic Ocean.

Scientists estimate that about 65 percent of the fish caught by the United States' commercial fishers and up to 70 percent of the fish living along the Atlantic coast of North America spend at least part of their life in Chesapeake Bay. About one-half of these fish spend their summers in the estuary. They arrive in the spring, feed on the bay's plentiful supply of plankton during the summer months, and then return to the open ocean in the autumn. The Chesapeake Bay estuary is also a popular spawning ground and nursery for many ocean fishes, but scientists aren't sure why. Do the young fish need to grow up in the estuary, or does the abundant food supply just make it a good choice? Perhaps one day researchers will be able to answer this important question.

LIVES INTERTWINED

Clearly, the estuary is an important place. Its three zones of salinity seem to be necessary for the different life stages of many fishes. For the estuary to remain healthy and balanced, the organisms in one zone depend on members of the other two zones.

Plants and benthic dwellers in the oligohaline zone rely on the nutrient input from fish that migrate from other zones during various stages of their life cycles. The nutrients come from waste material and from the remains of decaying, dead fish. Likewise, the mesohaline and polyhaline zones need energy input and nutrients from the oligohaline zone. These are provided by juvenile fish and other nektonic creatures as they move from less salty water toward saltier areas of the estuary.

All three zones rely on healthy plant growth. As the plants and other primary producers carry on photosynthesis, they add oxygen to the water. Without an adequate supply of oxygen, the water cannot support life. Currents that flow back and forth through the three zones ensure mixing. Thorough mixing prevents the water from becoming stagnant.

All living organisms in the estuary— from the tiniest copepod to the largest shark—depend on the estuary's system of checks and balances, provided by the food chain and the cycling of nutrients. Like a line of dominoes, if one part of the ecosystem fails and falls, a chain reaction occurs throughout the whole system. Maintaining the estuary's overall health requires a constant influx of nutrients and a continuous, even flow of energy between organisms. This occurs within each zone and back and forth among the three zones.

When only one species of plant or animal fills a specific niche, the chances of the ecosystem sustaining major damage if a problem occurs are much greater. The more diverse the estuary's living organisms are, the more likely it is that the ecosystem can restore its balance. For example, if one particular species of mud crab were to drop drastically in number, other crabs—or even small shorebirds—could scuttle in and help maintain the ecosystem while the distressed species recovered. This is why maintaining biodiversity is so important.

GREAT EGRET (ARDEA ALBA)

CHAPTER 6
PEOPLE AND THE CHESAPEAKE BAY ESTUARY

By now you know that a wide variety of organisms play important roles in the Chesapeake Bay estuary ecosystem. But did you know that people influence the ecosystem too? Our actions have a tremendous impact on the health and vitality of the estuary. Sometimes we do things that help the estuary, but sometimes we harm it.

People all over the world have built their homes and operated businesses near estuaries. Because estuaries are protected from the ocean's battering waves, they make excellent harbors for ships. The large

THE CHESAPEAKE BAY GETS ITS NAME FROM THE ALGONQUIN WORD *CHESEPIOOC*, WHICH MEANS "GREAT SHELLFISH BAY."

quantity of fish attracts fishers, who sell their catches to make a living.

Thousands of years before Europeans sailed into the waters of Chesapeake Bay, a number of Native American tribes lived near the bay's shores. They fished and hunted in the salt marshes and in the nearby deeper waters. The shellfish, fish, and land dwelling animals supplied them with plenty of food and materials for clothing. In fact, the Chesapeake Bay gets its name from the Algonquin word *chesepiooc*, which means "great shellfish bay." While the people in the Native American communities certainly used whatever they needed for their survival, they were careful not to take more than they could use within a certain time period, and they tried not to waste anything.

MARSH MASSACRE

When European explorers arrived in the 1400s, they were greatly impressed by the beautiful waters fringed with widespread salt marshes. The earliest explorers trapped and hunted with great success. Fishes, beavers, muskrats, elk, and other wildlife were plentiful. The explorers sailed back to Europe to sell their catches.

Later, settlers sailed across the Atlantic Ocean so they could have their own land. Many of the diaries kept by these people described the tremendous size of the salt marshes and the great bounty of fish and other wildlife in the bay. The settlers established towns close to the marshes, so they could graze their cattle, horses, and other livestock on the salt marsh grasses. A few coastal marshes in the Chesapeake Bay area are still used to graze animals today.

The Europeans did not think of the bay and the surrounding land in the same way as the Native Americans. The new settlers regarded wetlands as property that could be bought and sold. They quickly built homes and began farming. The settlers harvested the grasses, dried them, and then sold them as hay.

In the 1700s, people began to think of the estuary's salt marshes in yet another way. Instead of viewing them as an important source of hay, they began to see them as wastelands loaded with mosquitoes. For the next 200 years, people dumped soil, rock debris, and garbage into the salt marshes. The federal and state governments encouraged people to drain or fill in the marshes to create dry land for building. Homes, warehouses, factories, airports, and roads have gradually taken over former marshland.

OYSTERS IN DANGER

At the same time the bay's marshes were being destroyed, people were also harvesting untold numbers of shellfish, fish, and waterfowl from its waters. As the area's human population increased, so did fishing and hunting. The populations of some fishes and shellfish are now in serious jeopardy. One example is the American oyster.

When early navigators sailed into the bay, they often had difficulty steering their boats around the estuary's gigantic oyster beds. Now oysters are far from plentiful in the bay's waters. Between 1920 and 1980, an average of 27 million pounds (12 million kilograms) of oyster meat was harvested from the Chesapeake Bay each year. Then the oyster catch suddenly began to decline. In 1993, only 592,000 pounds (269,000 kilograms) of oyster meat was taken from the bay. The shellfish had been overharvested. The rate at which oysters were being removed from the bay exceeded the rate at which the remaining animals could reproduce and replenish the population. Scientists estimate the current oyster population is only 1 percent of what it was in early historic times.

Overharvesting is not the only reason that the bay's oyster population is dwindling. In the past few decades, pollution and construction projects have destroyed their habitat. And in the past 15 years, the population has been further reduced by two parasites that kill young oysters before they can reproduce.

Many people are concerned about the American oyster. They are working to protect and restore the bay's oyster population. They know that many of the estuary's inhabitants rely on oysters

MANY PEOPLE MAKE A LIVING FISHING IN CHESAPEAKE BAY AND ITS TRIBUTARIES.

and oyster bars for their survival. As oysters feed, they filter nutrients and materials out of the water. This helps keep the water clean. A single oyster can filter up to 1.3 gallons (5 liters) of water per hour. Scientists believe that several hundred years ago, the bay's oyster population could filter and recycle all the water in the bay in 3 to 4 days. Today, because the oyster population is so reduced, researchers estimate it takes about 1 year.

NUTRIENT NUISANCE

You might not think that what happens on farms and in forests hundreds of miles from the bay could affect the life of the estuary, but it does. When forests are cut down and fields are left bare, soil erodes. After it rains, the runoff washes large quantities of sediment into the streams and rivers. All that sediment eventually makes its way to the bay, where it blocks out the sunlight aquatic plants need for photosynthesis. Later, when the sediment settles to the bottom, it may suffocate bottom dwellers.

But that is not the only way that planting crops upstream from the bay can cause trouble. Farmers often use fertilizers

RUNOFF FROM AGRICULTURAL FERTILIZERS CAN CAUSE UNCONTROLLABLE ALGAL BLOOMS IN ESTUARIES.

CONSERVATIONISTS SOMETIMES PLANT GRASSES TO PREVENT EROSION. THIS MAN IS DRILLING HOLES IN THE SAND FOR THE GRASS HE WILL PLANT.

to help their crops grow. Most fertilizers contain large quantities of phosphorus and nitrogen—nutrients that stimulate plant growth. When rain washes fertilizers used in farmers' fields and on people's lawns into the estuary's watershed, it is only a matter of time before the nutrients end up in the bay. Nutrient-rich runoff from large livestock farms and sewage treatment plants also eventually makes its way to the bay.

When the nutrients enter the Chesapeake Bay estuary, algae growth explodes and the thick, dense mats block out the sunlight submerged aquatic vegetation (SAV) needs to survive. At one time, seagrass beds grew throughout the bay, but in the last 30 to 50 years, they have gradually shrunk. Some have disappeared completely.

Because people now recognize how important SAV is to the estuary ecosystem's health, they are working to improve water quality. Pollution controls on wastewater treatment and changes in construction practices and land usage patterns have helped make water conditions more favorable for SAV growth. So has a ban on phosphates in detergents, which often are flushed into wastewater systems. In addition, many farmers and homeowners have reduced the amount of fertilizer they use.

These measures have made a tremendous difference. Between 1978 and 1993, SAV in the Chesapeake Bay and its tidal tributaries increased from 41,748 acres to 73,092 acres (16,908 hectares to 29,602 hectares). By the 1990s, SAV beds were more abundant than they had been in the early 1900s.

A BULLFROG (RANA CATESBEIANA), COATED IN ALGAE

Unfortunately, the SAV comeback faltered in 1998. For some reason, the amount of seagrass declined by 8 percent. People are investigating why the reduction occurred and are monitoring the situation to make sure the decrease stops. Water management officials hope to reach their goal of 114,000 acres (46,200 hectares) of SAV by 2005. Will this goal be met? In large part, it depends on the efforts of the people who live in and visit the bay's watershed.

CHESAPEAKE BAY IS A BIRDWATCHERS' PARADISE.

FUN IN THE SUN

Over the years, people have used the Chesapeake Bay estuary for a variety of recreational activities. Birdwatchers enjoy observing the splendid array of waterbirds. Photographers and artists visit hoping to find the perfect picture. Hikers come to breathe in the tangy salt air as they explore marsh trails. Shell collectors sometimes find extra special treasures, such as fossilized shells, bones, and sharks' teeth, along the bay's tidal flats. Meanwhile, boaters enjoy cruising the estuary waters, and sport fishers face the challenge of catching striped bass, bluefish, sea trout, flounder, and drum.

When the sun goes down and it is time to eat, many people dine on the shrimp, oysters, clams, and crabs found in Chesapeake Bay. Nearly 50 percent of the United States's annual blue crab catch comes from the bay. When the estuary ecosystem is threatened, so are all the recreational pursuits of birdwatchers, photographers, artists, hikers, shell collectors, boaters, and fishers. As you can see, there are many important reasons to protect and preserve this precious estuary ecosystem.

CANADA GEESE *(BRANTA CANADENSIS)* AT SUNSET

WHAT YOU CAN DO

One of the best ways to learn about the Chesapeake Bay and other estuaries in the United States is by visiting them. Many estuaries have nature study programs and interpretive trails that teach people about the wildlife that lives there. Some also have boardwalks that crisscross a marsh, so you can look down and see all the wonderful things living there without trampling the plants or disrupting the animals. By staying on the boardwalks and trails, you can enjoy all the sights and sounds and know that you are causing no harm.

To protect the Chesapeake Bay and the many other estuaries along our coastline, we must make wise and informed choices about the role we will play in their future use. What can you do to protect estuary ecosystems? Here are some suggestions.

• Do not pour chemicals such as gasoline, paint, or household cleaners down the drains of sinks, tubs, or toilets. Also, do not pour them onto the ground or into a river or lake. They may seep into a groundwater system and pollute it. When the poisons come into contact with fish, they can kill them. Fish can also become poisoned by eating plants or animals that contain chemical poisons in their systems. Contact your local government and ask if they have a day designated for the safe collection and disposal of chemicals.

• Use safe alternatives to harsh household cleaners. Instead of commercial window cleaner, try a mixture of vinegar and water. Your windows will sparkle. A paste of baking soda and water effectively cleans sinks, tubs, and toilets.

• Do not throw trash and other garbage into rivers, lakes, bays, or the ocean. Not only are these things unsightly, but fish and other animals may eat pieces that make them sick. Some communities have water clean-up days. You might want to participate in one. If you do, be sure to do so with an adult's supervision and remember to wear gloves and boots.

• Do not trample or pull up plants in

marshes or along riverbanks. They are supplying animals with food and oxygen.

- Conserve water. It may not seem like much, but each time you get a drink and let the faucet run until the water gets cold, you are wasting water. Keep a water bottle in the refrigerator. And avoid letting the water run continuously while you are washing your hands and face or brushing your teeth.

- Take showers rather than baths. A typical bath uses at least 13 gallons (49 liters) of water. A typical shower uses less than half that amount.

- Learn what kinds of grasses survive best in your area. They will need less water and fertilizer to survive. Or consider planting flowers and shrubs that are native to your area as an alternative to a grassy lawn. Even scattered flowerbeds of native plants will make a difference.

- Use wood chips or bricks on pathways, rather than concrete. Rain can seep through wood chips or bricks and into the ground, resulting in less runoff. Less runoff means pesticides and fertilizers are less likely to find their way into streams and rivers.

- Collect rainwater in a barrel and use it to water plants around your house. Keep the barrel tightly covered when it isn't raining to prevent mosquitoes from laying their eggs in it.

- Join a community organization that takes an active role in estuary preservation and conservation.

YOU CAN BE INVOLVED IN FUTURE PLANNING

If you live in the Chesapeake Bay area, you can contact the Chesapeake Bay Program. This federally sponsored program was established in 1983 by the governors of Virginia, Maryland, and Pennsylvania and officials in the District of Columbia. The goals of the program include studying the bay ecosystem and implementing programs to protect it. The program offers a lot of information on the current health of the bay as well as information about the ongoing efforts of scientists, fishers, and other concerned people who want to maintain the estuary. In addition to the Chesapeake Bay Program, you can read newspapers and magazines to learn more about the bay. And don't forget to write letters to your state senators and representatives expressing your concerns and views about the Chesapeake Bay and its watershed. You can also send a letter to the governor of your state.

To write to the senators from your state:

The Honorable (name of your senator)
United States Senate
Washington, DC 20510

To write to your representative in Congress:

The Honorable (name of your representative)
U.S. House of Representatives
Washington, DC 20515

WEBSITES TO VISIT FOR MORE INFORMATION

The following websites contain a wealth of information. All suggest further web links for more information.

The Chesapeake Bay Program

<http://www.chesapeakebay.net>
This is the official website of the Chesapeake Bay Program. It provides information about the state of the bay, its watershed, and the flora and fauna that inhabit the estuary. It also features maps and a section on how to get involved in preservation and conservation.

Fragile Handle With Care

<http://www.dnr.state.md.us/bay/protect>
The Maryland Department of Natural Resources' site focuses exclusively on what individuals and children can do in their home, yard, and community to be environmentally responsible and help protect Chesapeake Bay.

National Estuary Program: Bringing Our Estuaries New Life

<http://www.epa.gov/owow/estuaries>
This site, which is sponsored by the U.S. Environmental Protection Agency, provides information about the National Estuary Program. It has links to all of the twenty-eight estuaries in the U.S. that belong to the program.

Potomac Adventure

<http://www.weta.org/potomac>
This site, which was developed and is maintained by the Washington Educational Telecommunications Association, Inc., focuses on ecosystems found along the Potomac River.

Susquehanna River Watch

<http://www.tier.net/riverwatch>
This site was created by teachers, students, and community volunteers and describes student monitoring projects along the Susquehanna River.

FOR FURTHER READING

Bell, David Owen. *Awesome Chesapeake: a Kid's Guide to the Bay*. Centreville, MD: Tidewater, 1994.

Fleisher, Paul. *Salt Marsh*. Tarrytown, NY: Marshall Cavendish, 1999.

Goodman, Susan E. *Wading into Marine Biology: Ultimate Field Trip 3*. New York: Aladdin Paperbacks, 2000.

Lippson, Alice. *Life in the Chesapeake Bay*. Baltimore, MD: Johns Hopkins Univ. Press, 1997.

McClung, Robert M. *Lost Wild America: The Story of Our Extinct and Vanishing Wildlife*. Hamden, Connecticut: Linnet Books, 1993.

Mills, Patricia. *On an Island in the Bay*. New York: North-South Books, 1994.

Patent, Dorothy Hinshaw. *Biodiversity*. New York: Clarion Books, 1996.

Rogers, Barbara Radcliffe. *An Adventure Guide to the Chesapeake Bay*. Edison, NJ: Hunter Publishing Company, 2001.

Scott, Michael. *Ecology*. New York: Oxford University Press, 1995.

VanCleave, Janice. *Ecology for Every Kid: Easy Activities that Make Learning About Science Fun*. New York: John Wiley & Sons, 1996.

Warner, William. *Beautiful Swimmers: Watermen, Crabs, and the Chesapeake Bay*. Boston: Little, Brown, 1994.

White, Christopher P. *Chesapeake Bay: Nature of the Estuary: A Field Guide*. Centreville, MD: Tidewater, 1989.

Whitman, Sylvia. *This Land Is Your Land: The American Conservation Movement*. Minneapolis: Lerner Publications Company, 1994.

Wright-Frierson, Virginia. *An Island Scrapbook: Dawn to Dusk on a Barrier Island*. New York: Simon & Schuster, 1998.

GLOSSARY

benthic: living on the bottom

biodiversity: the wide variety of life found in an ecosystem

biome: a type of naturally existing community of living organisms. Forests, wetlands, and lakes are all biomes.

decomposer: an organism that breaks down the remains of dead plants and animals

detritus: tiny materials found on the bottom of a body of water, such as bits of plants, animals, or rocks

ecosystem: a specific community of living organisms, the place they live, and the physical conditions that surround them. Chesapeake Bay and the Everglades are ecosystems.

estuary: the area where a river's mouth meets a bay or ocean and their waters mix

exoskeleton: an invertebrate's hard outer covering

food chain: a feeding order in which energy is passed from one living organism to another

glacier: a large, moving body of snow and ice

groundwater: water that sinks into the ground and flows inside the rock and soil

habitat: the area where an animal or plant lives, grows, and reproduces

headwaters: the place where a river begins

larva (pl. larvae): an early stage of development in the life of an animal such as a fish, insect, or crab

mesohaline zone: the area of an estuary with water that has a medium level of salinity

meteoroid: a small rocky or metallic object traveling through space. When it strikes a planet or other relatively large body, it is called a meteorite.

molt: to shed the exoskeleton as an invertebrate grows

nektonic: able to swim about freely, as fish and dolphins do

nursery: an area where young fish hatch and grow

nutrient: a substance, especially in food, that is needed for healthy growth

oligohaline zone: the area of an estuary with water that is either fresh or very low in salt content

photoplankton: tiny organisms that carry out photosynthesis and form the base of an estuary ecosystem's food chain

photosynthesis: the process plants and certain other organisms use to change sunlight, carbon dioxide, and water into energy in the form of sugars and starches

plankton: small, often microscopic, living organisms that float in water

polyhaline zone: the area of an estuary where the water is saltiest

precipitate: to form a solid that separates out of solution

primary consumer: an animal, such as a minnow, that eats primary producers

primary producer: a living organism, such as a plant, that carries out

photosynthesis to make food for itself

protoctist: a member of the group of simple living organisms that are not considered plants or animals

runoff: water that does not sink into the soil after rainfall or snowmelt

salinity: the amount of salt present in water

salt marsh: a saltwater wetland that is flooded for most of the year and contains a variety of grasses and small plants, but few trees

secondary consumer: an animal, such as an osprey, that eats other consumers

sediment: small pieces of rock, soil, and plant debris

tributary: a body of water that flows into a larger body of water

turbidity: the cloudiness of water

water column: a vertical section that extends through a body of water

watershed: the land area that supplies water to a river, lake, or bay

wetland: a place where the soil is moist for most or all of the year

INDEX

ABOUT THE AUTHOR

Sally M. Walker is the author of many books for young readers, including *Fossil Fish Found Alive: Discovering the Coelacanth* and the early reader *Mary Anning: Fossil Hunter*. When she isn't busy writing and doing research for books, Ms. Walker works as a children's literature consultant. She gives presentations at many reading conferences and has taught children's literature at Northern Illinois University. While she writes, Ms. Walker shares desk space with her family's two cats, who often jump onto the keyboard and contribute to manuscripts in progress. Ms. Walker lives in Illinois with her husband and two children.

PHOTO ACKNOWLEDGEMENTS

© Heather R. Davidson, cover, pp. 2–3, 25 (both), 26, 32, 50, 56, 59, 60 (right), 61, 62, 63; © Doug Sokell/Visuals Unlimited, p. 8; National Park Service, p. 11; © David W. Harp, pp. 12, 19, 21, 24 (both), 41 (both), 42, 45 (bottom), 47, 52, 60 (left); © Jack Dermid/Visuals Unlimited, pp. 17, 29; © David Wrobel/Visuals Unlimited, pp. 23, 35; © Rob & Ann Simpson/Visuals Unlimited, pp. 28, 51; © Mack Henley/Visuals Unlimited, p. 30 (left); © Gustav Verderber/Visuals Unlimited, pp. 30 (right), 31 (left), 40; © Joe McDonald/Visuals Unlimited, p. 31 (right); © Gerard Fuehrer/Visuals Unlimited, p. 33; © Dave B. Fleetham/Visuals Unlimited, p. 34; © Richard T. Nowitz/CORBIS, p. 37; © William C. Jorgensen /Visuals Unlimited, p. 39; © Patrice/Visuals Unlimited, p. 44; © C.P. Hickman /Visuals Unlimited, p. 45 (top); © Ken Lucas/Visuals Unlimited, p. 48; © Roger Cole/Visuals Unlimited, p. 49; © Lynda Richardson/CORBIS, p. 54